Foot Faults: Tennis Poems

Foot Faults: Tennis Poems

Sedarat

Roger ~~Federer~~

Dear Aimee,

I'm grateful to sign this book for a fellow player. I hope these poems inspire you as you compete for Two Bridges Tiger.

Much "Love" (pun intended),

[signature]

Published by David Robert Books

P.O. Box 541106

Cincinnati, OH 45254-1106

ISBN: 9781625492005

Poetry Editor: Kevin Walzer

Business Editor: Lori Jareo

Visit us on the web at www.davidrobertbooks.com

Acknowledgements:

"Opening a Can of Tennis Balls," *Form Quarterly* and *Journal of New Jersey Poets*; "Tennis Parents," *International Journal of Psychoanalytic Self-Psychology*; "Lines that End on my Backhand," *Ghazal Page*; "Playing the Older Gregarious Italian who Always seems to Win" and "Injury Report," *The Road Not Taken*; "When Gabriel García Márquez Played Tennis," *Atlanta Review*; "Upon the Weekend Warrior Taking Himself Entirely too Seriously," *Aethlon: Journal of Sports Literature.*

For players of all ages and skill levels.

Writing free verse is like playing tennis with the net down.
—Robert Frost

It's no accident, I think, that tennis uses the language of life. Advantage, service, fault, break, love, the basic elements of tennis are those of everyday existence, because every match is a life in miniature.
—Andre Agassi

Contents

Opening a Can of Tennis Balls

A sudden pop: the curved edge peeling back
Its metal tongue to let out a long sigh
About the loss of freshness and the lack
Of time before the bounce begins to die.
The empty can's inevitably blown
Onto the court just as a player serves,
As if to claim the balls it used to own,
A rolling, hollow trash talk that deserves
Foot stomps or sweeping underhanded hits
Along with frustrated eye rolls, head shakes
Denying that the thing's inanimate,
(Like it's intent on going up a break).
Abandoned by the fence after the match,
It props upright, pretending it's not trash.

Tennis

is
nets
n'
sets

Is
n't
it?

Origins of Tennis

for Glenn Burger

Monastic cloisters in the north of France,
Twelfth century. Bored with the same old psalm,
Monks grabbed a ball, invented *jeu de paume*.
Four hundred years of playing hurt their hands.

Voilà! They introduced the first racket.
Sure, first they merely hit against the wall,
But it looked like the sport they'd come to call
"*Tenez!*" before each serve over a net.

In 1850 when Charles Goodyear made
Bouncier balls, folks now could hit on grass.
Then Wingfield's court, shaped like an hour glass,
At country clubs came to displace croquet.

New rules were put in place at Wimbledon;
The redesigned rectangle court has stayed.
It starts in France, *mais je suis désolé.*
The modern game is really all England.

Tennis Types

The Pusher

An archetype on every public court,
He's mastered how to keep the ball in play.
Defensively, he redefines the sport,
Awaiting his opponent's next mistake.

Power Baseliner

Assured ground strokes will carry all her weight,
She takes a stand and whacks to claim each set.
Out of all players she has come to hate
The drop shot hustler who brings her to net.

Serve and Volleyer

Almost extinct as a spry dinosaur,
Beware of his approach. Sure, play your game
But with your racket as a gun. It's war
Against a charging beast (perfect your aim).

Moonballer

Balls hang so high you seem to have all day
To over-think, yet still somehow surprise
When they come down. Just try your best to play
Them in the air, or take them on the rise.

Upon the Weekend Warrior Taking the Game Entirely too Seriously

Ashamed, I must admit that tennis is
My life in middle age, though I'm not good
(I rarely follow through the way I should).
Before I play, that guy from Genesis
Inspires my stupid chores around the house.
While listening to "In the Air Tonight"
I step out into blinding grand slam light
And wave to all the center court applause.
But in reality I face the fear
Of dinking soft returns without much spin,
Dressed like a pro with brand new Wilson gear,
As if I didn't just learn this last year,
The basic backhand. Balls I hit loop in
So weak, even imagined fans don't cheer.

The Older Gregarious Italian who Always Seems to Win

Most players wouldn't play with him again.
He talks through games, and he's so passionate
His strong accent connects to every hit:
"I shoot'a 'da skeet. You know…clay pigeon!"
(He fires a forehand winner down the line).
"Next week I take 'a you to the Catskills.
 (He comes to net). "You have a gun?" (And kills
 My soft return).   "If not you use'a mine."
(When he attacks an overhead): "Let's a'
Suppose that ball, it was 'a 'da' target:
You take 'a the aim with my Beretta
And "Bang!" (the ball shoots by like a bullet).
"So I win 'da first and second set a.'
Do we play best a' five a'? I forget…"

That ball was in…

"No, just long."
"No, you're wrong."

"That's not fair!
I was there

On top of it
And didn't hit."

"Well, you should,
'Cause it was good."

"I made the call.
It's fifteen-all."

"Think you mean
Love-fifteen."

"God sees all.
He knows the ball

Wasn't in.
It's a sin

To say you know
When you don't."

"That's not fair.
It's in I swear."

"You're so wrong.
That ball was long."

Injury Report

Germán's out with a sprained elbow
And Daniel broke a rib.
Wes says his foot hurts, but I know
That he's been known to fib.

Bill M's a proven warrior,
I've seen him serve through pain
That paralyzed his right shoulder
And not even complain.

I saw an orthopedist
For some old knee troubles.
"You're old," he said, and I got pissed.
He told me to play doubles.

By far my greatest injury
The only time I've cried
(On my way home; No one could see)
Was over my hurt pride.

Professional Regret

"I wish I would have been a tennis pro,"
My friend Paul tells me when we're hitting balls.
"In mid-life crisis now, some things I know
I wish I would have been. A tennis pro
Lives on his past at country clubs as coach."
With no retirement plan, I covet Paul's.
"I wish *I* would have been a tennis pro,"
I tell my friend as we keep hitting balls.

The Tennis Parents

The tennis parents offer their young kids
Up to the sport: self-centered sacrifice
In service of their grand slam hopes and dreams.

Shrinks use the "superego vs. id"
As model to umpire and analyze
The tennis parents offer: their young kids'

Will sublimated into overheads
And backhands/forehands forced inside the lines
(In service of their grand slam hopes). And dreams

Reveal years later damage that they did.
(In therapy they have to pay the price).
The tennis parents offered their young kids

Brings hard returns they never expected
As they hold their own rackets with surprise
In service of their grand slam hopes and dreams.

Life as a zero sum game, frustrated
Adulthood without play becomes the prize
The tennis parents offer their young kids
In service of their grand slam hopes and dreams.

Eye on the Ball

"An exercise in seeing," says the book.
"You have to train your eyes to catch the brand
Of ball regardless of its spin. Don't look
Elsewhere." I fix my gaze upon "Wilson"
But Wes is wearing his retro headband
As if we're in the *Royal Tenenbaums.*
He strokes his hipster beard between his serve
Like he's relaxed, then fires a Sampras bomb
That whizzes by me as a yellow blur.
Few things in tennis are as they appear.
You do your best to focus on your play
Despite performances of your partner
Or what the stupid how-to books might say.
Like everyone I try to use my eyes;
Improve as I anticipate surprise.

Days without Tennis

Without a partner you start to withdrawal,
At best serve solo, hit against the wall.
True addicts sometimes order the "Lobster"
(High-priced returns—the same old sob story).
But rain's the worst. When you're priced out of clubs
Live tennis on TV somehow just rubs
It in your face, yet still you sit and watch,
Pretending that it's you who plays the match.

The Sufi Tennis Player

His right arm raised like a dervish
in old days of the Persian court
he smacks a serve with so much spin
the ball's a blurry whirl of whoosh
the racket hammer thwacked
in Rumi's marketplace staccato
footwork baseline squeaks
dances to net angles of tension
played from a place beyond
knowing through training
clinics coaches agony
of wins and losses the ball
reduced to petty ego netted
over-headed unforced errors
(the goddamn sun without a visor!)
until new game set match
backhand back in the zone
of easy shots and aces
Wilson stamped across the ball
transcendent as a mystic's prayer.

Hapward's

A house converted to a tennis shop:
Victorian two-story, racket frames
Along the walls in place of portraits.
Adidas shirts and shorts on hangers haunt
The rooms like ghosts of headless players ranked
In stature, rows of colorful new shoes
(their fancy footwork all laid out for them).
The old guy with the bowl hair cut walks in,
A tireless tennis Yoda who can match
Each player to a racket since the days
Of wooden serve and volley on the grass,
Yet reconnects now in the modern age:
String tensions, grips and compositions for
The average rec. hitter and pro.
By far the coolest thing about the place
Is that it's buried deep within Bloomfield
In a forgotten Jersey neighborhood.
It's best to know someone who's been before,
Able to lead you back here like it's home.

Coaches

Amir one summer taught me follow through
By showing him my handle's "W."

That fall in an advanced adult ed. clinic.
This old pro shot me down (burned out cynic).

Then in a winter class I took indoors
John showed me how to whack ground strokes with
force.

A college kid in spring became the best.
He taught me more, while charging me much less.

Next year I hired one meaner than them all.
He screamed, "Hey Grandma, don't just push the ball!"

Grand Slams

Australian Open

The Aussies so revere the sport
Arenas stand for players, which
Would matter more on Margaret's Court
If it were not for Djokovic.

Wimbledon

The balls have never moved so fast
But English manners still define
How players dress and act on grass
While ripping clean hits down the line.

French Open

Roland Garros is ruled by Spain.
So? *C'est la vie*, as the French say.
Nadal enjoys the longest reign.
But his feet too are made of clay.

U.S. Open

The anti-Wimbledon, it's hard
Court matches nights at Arthur Ashe.
An underdog or wildest card
Provokes a fifth set drunken bash.

Playing through Impossible Weather

Too humid. Running for balls makes us sick.
Our only weekend free. What can we do
But force ourselves to move through air so thick
It hurts to breathe? One summer in Chengdu
On our far eastern honeymoon we watched
Two players sweat it out through hell. "God how
Can they survive this five set sewer match?"
Asked my hot wife. Well, I can tell her now,
I think, assuming I survive heat stroke.
Between games Daniel says he sees bright light.
"You're center court at a grand slam." The joke
Would not go over on that sticky night.
I can't recall the score. Think I lost it.
I just remember feeling exhausted.

In Response to Jay, the Poet's Godson, Claiming that Tennis is just for Rich Snobs

The world is on the court
But occupied by Slavs
Who've colonized the sport,
A metaphor for "haves"/-
"have-nots" with corporate
Endorsements like a CHASE⊙
Stamped on the net, logo-
Centric reformations
Of capital reclaimed
By post commie-nations
Who've learned to play the game.

Playing Indoors

A readjustment of both time and space,
Lobs hit the ceiling and resist your chas-

Ing down (helped by a wall). The toughest gets
Push you beyond the alleys to the nets

That separate each court. The loud echo
Of racket pops and conversations blow

Your concentration. Price per hour's a bitch
(More proof this sport belongs just to the rich).

Still, knowing outside courts have turned to ice,
You must admit that playing inside's nice.

The Chef

The chef's so serious. He doesn't speak.
A few games in I let him in my head.
My serves turn soft; my forehand is so weak
He burns returns and slices me at net.
My goose is cooked. The worst match of my life
First freezes me with fear, then boils me o-
Ver when I unforce error. His sharp knife
Skills cut off angles. I don't even know
Where I can place the ball. His stoic gaze
Won't break. You'd think at 52 he'd ease
Up on me some. His last serve is an ace,
A statement on his hard court masterpiece.
"I'm not that good," he says. "You could've won."
"Just stick a fork in me," I sigh. "I'm done."

On the Coach Asking for our Court after only Half an Hour

Pro coaches are a dime a dozen.
You'd think that he would understand
Humility and not demand
A public court. (Alas, he doesn't).

He interrupts me as I serve.
"Okay guys. Almost time to quit?"
You've had your fun. It's etiquette."
This jackass has a lot of nerve.

"It's our first set!" my partner cries.
 The other players stop and stare.
"This interrupting isn't fair!"
(His waiting student rolls his eyes).

He leaves himself deep in our heads.
I double fault, unforce error,
Replay the moment in terror,
Obsess on what I should have said.

Lines that End on my Backhand

To learn how to depend on my backhand
I wrote three steps in pen on my backhand:

"First plant your foot, then drop the head, and fol-
Low through!!!" (Emphatic end on my backhand).

I have to brush the ball instead of push
To generate topspin on my backhand.

Goddamn, why do I lock my arms and swing!?
I need to put some bend on my backhand.

Before I stand a chance against Daniel,
I have to learn to win on my backhand.

"You baby hitter! No one swings like that."
(The sound of me hatin' on my backhand).

There goes another game. What can I do?
A ball netted again on my backhand.

"Be patient, Roger. Learn to trust your swing
And plant that foot!" Coach Ben, on my backhand.

Leaving his Wife for Tennis Camp

Why wouldn't she resent his excess tennis?
Kids starting school and her work piling up
And once again he chooses to disrupt
Routine. "It's like you're off to see your mistress,"
She tells him as he packs his sleeping bag.
"You like her more than me!" He lets it go
Because he'll soon find comfort on the courts
(He plans to hit all day until it hurts).
"You watch it there! Don't think that I don't know
There's little hotties in cute tennis skirts.
You better not play nights with them indoors.
Keep your own balls inside your cold cabin.
I mean if you so much as even flirt
Stay in the Catskills with your tennis whores;
Ask if they're really worth the fun you're havin.' "

Do Tennis Players Get the Yips?

Of course there's always some mis-hits
When warming up. But if third set
Returns still sail into the net
You're jinxed. Though not as bad as golf,
The double faults seem just as aw-
Ful as when missing some dumb putt.
Worse players start to kick your butt.
Each error makes you over-think.
Forget the coach. You need a shrink.

Famous People who Play(ed) Tennis

Stars now don't seem so bright. Just "Friends" we know
From reruns (Perry, Cox, and L. Kudrow).
Next to late greats there's no comparison.
Consider Redford, Rogers, or Hepburn.
Among prose writers there is no lack of
Incredible examples: Nabokov
And Joyce in doubles versus Martin Amis
Paired with the daunting David Foster Wallace.
The poets? They just play with metaphor
(Like Frost); don't even know how to keep score.

Saying Goodbye to my old Djokovic Shoes

One year and all front tread is gone.
I've washed the inserts. They still smell.
Since clay court matches, when I put them on
Red clouds rise up. My feet in hell
Of ripped out souls. (I've tried strong glue;
It doesn't last). They lost their squeak
From footwork on hard courts. One shoe
Tongue's frayed as if it tries to speak
But can't. The Arabs have a word
For objects given character
By long term use. This loss must hurt
Because I know the wear and tear
Belongs to my long-blistered calloused feet
That suffer from so much painful defeat.

A Few Lines from the Old School Court Philosopher

Ghosts with wood rackets on the grass
Remind us of what we'd forget:
Their charming rallies at the net,
An all too sanitary past.

***

They've done away with tennis whites.
There's color now at Wimbledon.
Old purists bleach or put tape on
All logos and zig-zaggy stripes.

***

It once was a gentleman's game
Before the fist pumps and trash talk,
Grandstanding for crowds like a cock.
Since Connors this sport's not the same.

Foot-Working from Byzantium

This is no doubles court for younger men.
Germán and I play seventy-year olds:
Tall Brit at net, small baseline Indian.
Their serves are not that strong, but each one holds
His game. Then they break ours, a timeless win.
Germán says it's because we're fighting colds.
"Come on," I say, "We both have to admit,
We're younger, but they're more mentally fit."

An aging tennis player's inspiring
For what he fights against. They moved with grace
And struck tight angles, even while limping
Between each point, their knees and elbows braced
Like exo-skeletons, decay preserved:
Batman's grandfather seeking his revenge
On loss of youth, inverted justice served
And volleyed at young punks. We came unhinged
By their mental conditioning: Decades
Of focus we can't match, which never fades.

Oh tennis maestros making your last stand
Like battle-proven generals on the field,
Sprint for short balls, lean into your forehand,
Show weekend warriors power that you wield.
Yeats trash talked you (he could be such a dick).
Old age, he claimed, at best rests within art.
If he had balls he would've grabbed a stick
Instead of his lame pen and served with heart
Despite the thought of self as museum,
Foot-working out of old Byzantium.

Tennis Geometry

Let **A B**all **C**rosscourt land somewhere random.
The series of rectangles painted white
Connect three points upon a plane, invite
An application of well-known theorems.
Still, studying geometry's no use
Toward reaching some elusive mastery.
I doubt Nadal can tell you his degree
Of angles based on a hypotenuse.
But in an age reducing sports to stats
There must be something for math dorks to find
By substituting rackets for wood bats.
The sharpest volley winner always adds
To 180, a triangle outlined
By that Greek player called Pythagoras.

Impressionistic Serves

They just painted his courts reddish-tan as
His new deck stain. He goes to play this fall,
Just as the maple leaves come down, canvas
His charming town. He serves ball after ball,
Sees yellow-green dots dribble outside lines,
His racket-brush now Jackson-Pollockesque,
Reframing arbitrary dropped designs.
There's order, of course, in what's chaotic,
But no one's here to see. If art happens
Without an audience, does it exist?
What if he's not an artist, just intends
To take a break from chores and play tennis?
It's silly asking this late in the day.
The court at sunset looks like a Monet.

Winning Ugly

Brad Gilbert calls it stepping on his throat:
The close out of a match when you're ahead.
It's less technique and more a state of mind,
A different kind of footwork when the foot
Figuratively lands upon the throat,
The double metaphor of spongy lungs
Collapsing under pressure of your toes.
I quickly get the concept in my head
But can't quite send the message to my foot.
(Like when you watch a pro hit hard forehands
Then try returning that same hard forehand).
I've been up 5-4 then fell on my ass.
I start to choke, cut off air to my brain.
Then some opponent steps upon *my* throat.

Inner Dialogue

You're player 1 *and* player 2
In matches for and against you.

Unforced errors, hit long or wide?
Your true opponent's on your side

Trash thinking stupidest mistakes:
"You'll never win; you're down two breaks."

He knows the worst you've ever felt
And starts to hit below the belt:

"Hey ace, you don't serve how you should.
Easy returns mean you're no good

Like your performance on the job.
Look at the way you grandma lob;

No wonder you don't earn respect
And your financial life is wrecked."

The Zen-solution's to observe
What player two does with the serve

Without judging the swing or toss,
Less driven coach or awful boss

And more Buddha whose gentle facts
Improve your game as you relax.

On Getting Incredibly Close to a Side Court Match at the US Open

For Ryan Black

While eating chicken with Tabasco
A serve with so much heat flew toward my face
I swear I swung my drumstick. "Verdasco!"
The Spaniards cried. It felt like I'd been aced
Next to the unranked Russian, more proof of
What David Foster Wallace said about
Live tennis versus TV: it's true love
Compared with porn. I almost got thrown out
At first set point for arguing a call
Against the favorite. "Shhh...*Cállate!*"
Fans swore as their Verdasco held the ball.
I shut up when I saw security,
Assured I did everything I could do
To help my Russkie get the W.

Drop Shot

A drop shot's slo-mo
Suspension of warped time.
You think "run" but don't go,
Negating body-mind

Connection. Spins and plays
With you, but isn't fair;
Promises endless days
Like life— then just dies there.

Tennis to Go

Poor Amit never got his MBA.
He failed his overachieving parents
(The typical accomplished immigrants)
And had to learn to make it his own way.

With only forced mastery of tennis,
Seed money from his uncle, and contacts
Throughout the suburbs of Connecticut's
.1%, he made his own business

Delivering hot twenty-something pros
To wealthy housewives and their horny men,
A service to rec. players' temptation
That promised huge returns. "Tennis to Go's

The Hooters of the ivy league," he told
His golfing friends, a quasi-Midas man
Who knew enough of supply and demand
To turn a sexy rich sport into gold.

Tennis in Heaven

Hey Preacher, *is* there tennis in heaven?
Why fear death if there's tennis in heaven?

Let Dante tour with masters throughout hell;
I'll take amateur tennis in heaven.

Make sure to pray for rackets and a court
Or we'll just play air tennis in heaven.

Let angels line judge and umpire each match,
Insuring that it's fair tennis in heaven.

Opponents bless you as they beat you down.
Tough love. *C'est la guerre*! Tennis in heaven.

For God's sake Gabriel. Don't hog our courts.
They're public! We share tennis in heaven.

Late greats might try to dictate your match pace.
Don't let them play *their* tennis in heaven.

On Seeking Revenge in Intermediate Tennis Clinic

There was a Brit player named Neil
Who took me down 40 to nil.
He said I can't hit,
So I called him a shit,
Then served at his balls till he kneeled.

Ball Jokes (Actual conversations heard or participated in on court)

Player #1: Do you need another ball?
Player#2: No, I have two.

Player #1: These are shitty balls.
Player #2: Sorry, I always have shitty balls.

Player#1: I thought you were bringing balls?
Player#2: I had balls, but my wife played with them.
Player#1: I wish my wife would play with my balls.

Player#1: I brought a sack of balls
Player #2: A ball sack?

Player#1: Are you putting that ball down your shorts?
Player#2: Yeah, I don't have pockets.
Player#1: Dude, I don't want to touch your sweaty balls.

Tennis Don'ts

Don't worship trophies you've earned on your shelf.
You ultimately play against yourself.

Don't argue if the ball was on the line.
Remember: a good partner's hard to find.

Don't buy a racket used by Federer.
It really can't help you play much better.

Don't disrespect a player who's not fit.
You'll be surprised how well the big guys hit.

On Going through the Stages of a Loss

So what? The other guy was really good.
And no, you really didn't play that well.
Like Meryl Streep's performance in *Silkwood*
Go take a violent shower, scrub the hell
Of toxic loss away. Then start to pass
Through every stage of grief, from denial
Into acceptance that he kicked your ass.
The anger's tough. When I lose to Daniel
I think of poems I mis-edited
And get a little jealous of his fame,
Replaying all the backhands I netted
On lost ad points during each crucial game.
In writing this, I'm still stuck on stage two[1].
So who am I to tell you what to do?

---

[1] Anger

Forget the Score

Okay you're up. Remember how you swore
No matter what that you'd forget the score?

It's you against yourself, an ego war.
Surrender as you let go of the score.

Play tennis to play tennis. Know the more
You Zen your game, the less you're keeping score.

John: "Win or lose, when you get in your car
Leave your last match behind. Forget the score."

Who cares? Poe's Raven's famous "Nevermore"
Caws for how long they'll recollect your score.

The Troubadours of Tennis

The troubadours of tennis fought for wit
As much as points, as if they played the court-
Ly love tradition as they played doubles,
Though only the lit. critic had this sense
Of his crew's humorous and vulgar verse
Around the net throughout their heated match.

Most nights under the lights there was no match
For his screenwriter-partner's well-trained wit.
He hit back balls in time like measured verse
While telling stories to crack up the court
About life in L.A. "Such lyric sense,"
Observed the critic, "Like his racket doubles

As lyre." Ironically their main doubles
Opponent played guitar, which set the match
To music in a metaphoric sense
Like literal bards battling their wit
For sparrow-hawks awarded by the court.
The tension of the net rewrote past verse

Above their heads, arched lobs as meta-verse
Retracing past bird-flight. Each line doubles
As postmodern invention of the court.
So what if this symbolic tennis match
Got lost on them. By trying to outwit
Each other they translated the essence

Of literature's "historical sense"
Defined by T.S. Eliot where verse
Is timeless. Whether authors now know it
A single work they think they write doubles

Upon another, playing a tough match
Of inter-textual tennis, the court

Designed by Bakhtin from another court.
The reader at this point must get a sense
Of poetry as surface-level match.
The forehand of the poet foregrounds verse
Against tradition, where rhyme scheme doubles
As his attempt to win at serving wit:
A
C
E

At Net

i.

We	Whack
Hit	Back
And	Forth
Run	Split
Step	Step
Cross	The
Court	Court

ii.

Love	Love
Game	Game
Set	Set

t
i
e
b
r
e
a
k

Win	Loss

iii.

So much underspin
the ball clears the net...bounces
back all by itself.

iv.

```
        ( )
      ( ) N ( )
    ( )    E    ( )
  O        T        O
```

Tough Guy Tennis

Breaking court etiquette shirtless Justin
uber-athlete pre-match juicer
swears like a sailor the pee-wee clinic
two courts over not his fucking problem.
A Jersey guy teeth capped pecks tatted
thirty-nuttin instead of love
'cause love is weak the married woman
with a rock the size of a tennis ball
bent over her own Mercedes another one
who pays the bills so he can bike
and run crunch abs ad infinitum.
"We're animals!" He growls post-rally
4 hours into a 5 setter. "Beast!" he screams
after hard fought backhand winners.
If I'm up but unforce error: *Ah....!*
You just let me through the doggy door!
His index finger waving like De Niro.
Don't tell me the suburbs make you soft
when I dive on asphalt to return
his monster serve bruise ribs
bloody my forearm want my wife
for a moment even my mom
but when he comes to help me up
tell him *Get back to your side*
Bitch this ain't over it's just begun.

Most Tennis Players Internalize a Merciless Father

Of course the twin boys play for their old man.
I watch them watch him after each point made
In hope he'll look up from his *New York Times*.
Why can't I focus on my own damn game?
They're always one court over from my match,
These brothers fighting for conditioned love.
(It's like Freud fated them to reappear).
Once I decided it was in my head
And almost didn't care about the pain
I heard in all their Cain and Abel fights
Along respective baselines. As I walked
Off court I met him at the gate. "Your kids
Kick ass out there." I said. A dad myself,
I can't help liking when my pride is fed.
"I don't know what you're even doing here,"
He told me with a frown. "It makes me tired
Just watching your unstructured defense play."
Before I could say something offensive
About his stealing his kids' childhood years
He drove his little Agassis away.

When Gabriel García Márquez played tennis...

the ball hung overhead in humid air,
his index finger directing flight
beyond tropical birds he knew by name,
over Macondo trees, their roots stretched
through centuries, winding like tendrils
of syntax across the rain forest
where ghosts of guerilla fighters machete
into sugarcane and wildflowers, a palette
of blood-syrup over crushed ice
at carnivals, children with tails swinging
from branches, their mouths stretching
down like the ball the old man smashes
open at last, sending a yellow army
of butterflies into the mountains,
an Aracataca sunset hatched
from the frenzied racket
in the author's mind.

Bradford Family Court in Brandreth, NY

So many weeds on court we need Round Up
To play, I joke. "Pretend it's Wimbledon,"
Says Colin. Like the concrete, we crack up.
There's valleys near the net. The balls roll in
And die, a trick drop shot for our mini-
Ten-minute tennis. Drilling for the match
I volley into valleys, more mini-
Golf but [putt] when in Rome...or in Brandreth.

It's no Arcadia, but horses neigh
When Colin whacks a serve. Back in real life
He's an economist. Here he can play
Both mountain man and doubles with his wife.
Third set at sunset and "The Fox" appears:
His transgendered daughter, my closest friend;
I named her that not so much for her beard
But for her sly antics (they never end).

Her old man beats me. I'm ashamed of course.
But once, when playing H.O.R.S.E with Fox she set
Me straight: "You lose, but get to be the horse."
I think of this, while shaking hands at net
And watching a real horse come to the fence.
He doesn't care a bit about a win,
Just eats his grass: pastoral difference
Between my ego-centric fight and Zen.

Goodbye to the Late Greats

The circuit that they play winds down so fast
The best get hurt as they start to grow old.
Their wrists, like fame, were never meant to last
(Strokes fall apart, the servers cannot hold).
It's rare to find a pro like Agassi
Who reinvents himself for a comeback:
Aced mullet, wife accepting him as he
Appears, and acupuncture for his back.
The sport grows younger, I get more depressed.
All my contemporaries have retired.
And some look so much older, like Sampras.
To think these were the guys I once admired
Means I too now belong in the past tense
And sadly may have played my last tennis.

First Snow upon Mountainside Courts

Balls lying buried here have long been dead.
All line-defining tension's now erased,
And rows of nets seem random, out of place,
As snowflakes put the rectangles to bed.

This week I learned that Justin passed away,
O.D.'ing in the shower. Thirty-eight
And in ridiculously perfect shape.
He called us animals, howled as we played

Hard on these courts directly in the sun
For hours without a break. We knew we hit
Defensively, but didn't give a shit
Since Jersey guys like us were born to run.

He sounds so tough, but he only played mean.
The rare times I took him, he'd come to net
To bear hug me; my shirt drenched in his sweat
And grease from pecks he'd rub with Vaseline.

Another friend, back in the late 80's,
Convinced we live through others when we go,
Taught me to leave the world with love. I know
He stayed with me after he died of AIDS

Like Justin will in spring back on our court.
I'll see him screaming "Beast!" and pump his fist,
When I chase down a ball and dive for it.
Somewhere beyond this fence he'll know he's heard.

Last Serve

for Steve Sussmann

I'm serving solo just like how I'll die:
With no one but me looking at my faults.
The setting's perfect, since in deep fall it's
The end of free court time, which means that I
Am left just hanging on to what I've learned
This summer: how to toss and flick the wrist
For power, and just what good placement is.
I hold my own with better players, earned
Respect that makes them stand at the baseline.
Of course once I begin to ace the game
There's no one to play me, almost the same
As when you pass away. At last you find
Life's more about process than keeping score.
What matters when you're put to final rest
Is knowing for yourself you did your best.

ABC's of Tennis Greats

Arthur Ashe

Ashe's accomplishments always awe:
Australian, American, and Anglican awards;
Anti-apartheid and AIDS activist.

Andre Agassi

All along answering aces,
an agonized adolescence
ate away at adulthood.

Tracy Austin

An accident atrophied
another a-typical
adolescent achiever.

Boris Becker

"Boom Boom" Boris.
[*Der'*] bomber.
Barron [von Slam].

Don Budge

Before Budge
babies
bobbled balls.

Björn Borg

Bow-legged beast.
Best baseliner
beyond belief.

Jennifer Capriati

Child champion.
Court crusher.
[In]credible career

Michael Chang

Countered cramps.
Conquered conventional
court chasers.

Kim Clijsters

Consistently court-capable.
C+ confidence.
(*C'est la vie*).

Jimmy Connors

Cocky
comeback
champion.

Jim Courier

Courageously
conquered
Connors.

Margaret Court

Court champion.
Crazy Christian conservative
criticizing celebrated cultures.

Lindsay Davenport

Dauntingly
developed
dynamo.

Novak Djokovic

Dominant
deliveries
don't joke.

Stefan Edberg

Even entrenched
[in an] exceptional era,
excellently excelled.

Roy Emerson

"Emmo" exponentially
exploded
every event.

Chris Evert

Earned
everyone's
envy.

Roger Federer

Friendliest fighter.
Fantastically famous.
Federer forever!

Althea Gibson

[Inte]grated grandly,
garnered grandeur,
golfed.

Steffi Graf

Grand [s]lam
German
greatness.

Justine Henin

Height hampered,
hard hits humbled
heavy hitters.

Lleyton Hewitt

Hard
hustling
hell hound.

Martina Hingis

Held
historically
high honors.

Billie Jean King

King
Kong
killer.

Rod Laver

Reaped rewards.
Repeated records.
Really remarkable run.

Ivan Lendl

[B] liner
leveling
losers.

Amélie Mauresmo

Marvelously
Murdered many.
Mentored Murray.

John McEnroe

Masterful moxie.
Manly mojo
muscled matches.

Andy Murray

Meanest
match
mate.

Martina Navratilova

No-nonsense
never-ending
natural.

Fred Perry

Premiere [across the]
                    pond
player.

Andy Roddick

Really
ripped
rallies.

Pete Sampras

Seriously
strong
serve.

Monica Seles

Single's slammer
Steffi's supportive stalker
slashed.

Maria Sharapova

Severely
spirited
swinger.

Bill Tilden

Topped tennis.
Transgressed
teenagers.

Mats Wilander

Wonderful winner
(without
Wimbledon).

Serena Williams

Superior Whacker.
Supreme Winner.
Superwoman.

Venus Williams

Voluminous Wingspan.
Violent Whacks.
(Very Williamsesque).